T0381338

My Boy Jesus

JOSEPH'S STORY

WRITTEN BY

TED EREKSON

ILLUSTRATED BY MEG EREKSON

Order this book online at www.trafford.com
or email orders@trafford.com

Most Trafford titles are also available at major online book retailers.

Printed in the United States of America.

ISBN: 978-1-4669-0220-6

Library of Congress Control Number: 2011919258

Trafford rev. 03/01/2012

 www.trafford.com

North America & international
toll-free: 1 888 232 4444 (USA & Canada)
phone: 250 383 6864 ♦ fax: 812 355 4082

Foreword

I have always wondered what Joseph, the stepfather of Jesus, felt as he experienced the life of Jesus.

In relating this story I do not claim any revelation concerning the events in this account. The only true source is in the scriptures, which tell little of Joseph's feelings, and only vaguely share with us the simple facts of events.

I have used my limited knowledge of the Jewish way of life at the time of Joseph and Mary, my emotions and feelings as a father, and I have made some assumptions about some of the experiences Joseph and Jesus may have had to compile this account.

What I hope to accomplish is for you to know that Joseph had feelings of a loving father for his Stepson, he knew that Jesus was the Son of God, and his experiences with Him were precious.

Ted Erekson

Originally told and written Christmas 1998

This book is dedicated to our grandkids
Toad and Yeti.
It is also dedicated to all our future
grandkids just waiting to come down
from heaven.

Acknowledgements

I would like to first and foremost thank my Heavenly Father for the gift of being able to share stories with others. My wife Meg and I have been dreaming about publishing this book for years and now the dream has come true. Every word and every drawing has been an inspiration and has touched us deeply, as well as all the friends and family that have seen and heard and felt it.

Thanks to all those that encouraged us to make this book a reality; our kids, Izaak, Rachaal, and Ishmaal and many friends and family members, as well as my storytelling fans.

We would also like to especially thank our daughter-in-law, Vanessa, for really motivating us to get this done!

My Boy Jesus

JOSEPH'S STORY

Christmas. . . I have seen your day and have seen what you call Christmas. You frantically worry and run to and fro preparing, gathering together, and spending hours at what we in my time call a market place or bazaar. It is all bizarre to me, this fast paced life of yours. You spend your earnings as if there is no tomorrow and justify debt as though it was necessary.

My name is Joseph of Nazareth. I am a carpenter. I come to you from the past of over 2000 years. Let me tell you what Christmas was really like and what my boy, Jesus, meant to me.

She was my best friend. Her penetrating eyes were the color of polished cedar. Her skin was the soft and silky texture of olive wood. Her hair would blow in the wind like the tendrils of honeysuckle. When she smiled my heart would stop and my whole soul would smile back.

Mary. . . I didn't need Gabriel to tell me that she was chosen! We used to go for walks in the hills on the outskirts of Nazareth and sit and talk for hours.

We would joke about being cousins (everyone in Israel was cousins) and we would make light of the fact that growing up our parents would tell us we were of royal lineage, from David himself.

We would talk of me building a grand palace for our royal offspring to live in. Then we would laugh and know that the simple life is what we truly desired.

The day we were betrothed was the best day of my life. Mary glowed with the light that comes from someone pure and beautiful.

Betrothal was more than getting engaged in your day. We publicly made sacred promises to each other under a canopy, and the only way to break such a commitment was to file a writ of divorcement. The culmination of this sacred event was the actual marriage, which would take place at a later date.

The timing was perfect! I had to complete a home I was building for Ezra the tent maker and Mary wanted to go and visit her cousin Elizabeth. Elizabeth was with child, which was extremely strange in that she was an old woman and the events surrounding the pregnancy were beyond explanation.

She was gone only 3 months, which was an eternity not to be able to hear her laugh and watch her eyes sparkle.

I missed Mary terribly!

When she returned, Mary had changed. I wasn't sure if it was for good or bad, but she seemed thoughtful and like she needed to talk. I stopped working on the job and we headed for the hills to our favorite patch of grass surrounded by lilies.

She started talking and all I remember clearly is "... I am with child". I was numb. Didn't she know I loved her with all my soul? I vaguely remember her saying an angel came and declared unto her great things concerning the child . . .The angel's name was . . . Gabriel.

Every step going back to the village my feet got heavy, and all around me was slow moving. As we parted, she whispered, "I love you." I watched as she walked away. She still looked as pure and beautiful as the day we were betrothed.

The law! The cursed law required that I deal with this situation. I could have her judged publicly . . . and they would stone her. I could privately put in a writ of divorcement, but with an explanation . . . they would stone her. Time stood still as I pondered over these things. As I buried my face in my hands and wept I felt a calmness come over me. I laid down and rested my eyes and a dream opened up to me.

It was real . . . yet unreal.

An angel came to me and told me that Mary's child was of God, the Chosen One, the Messiah. He informed me that I was to marry my betrothed immediately and raise the child as my own.

I didn't sleep well that night I was so excited.

When I saw Mary the next morning, she looked up and knew that I understood. We ran and held each other. This was right. The warmth that passed through us told me this was right.

We were married at once!

Her small frame swelled as the babe within her grew. My heart jumped when the tiny figure within her kicked as my rough, calloused hand felt Mary's belly.

Oh, we loved each other as much as Abraham and Sarah.

Then again my peace was challenged! The scoundrel Augustus decreed all the Jews be counted and taxed in the land of their fathers.

Yes, we went to Bethlehem together. Mary begged me to take her. She was heavy with child and in no condition to travel, but she could convince me to part the Red Sea and I would oblige.

Mary came on the journey without one complaint, although I could see her discomfort as we bumped along the stone strewn road.

No room anywhere! There were so many people . . . thousands! I was desperate. I pounded on the heavy oak door of the inn furthest from town.

"No room!" . . . his brow was downturned and firm. As he said it, he saw Mary holding her belly as if she were holding a baby in her arms. His brow softened and he raised his hands and motioned for us to follow.

As he showed us the meager accommodations I thought to myself, "No, not here." But it was all there was in town. I nodded and he left us with a small oil lamp. I unpacked our blankets, piled and fluffed some hay for Mary, and we immediately fell asleep as we lay down for the night.

"Joseph . . . ," her voice was soft and demanding. I looked at her face in the bluish moonlight and saw a seriousness about her.

It was time!

I wanted to run out. You see, Jewish men are not trained in the birthing of children. Also, under strict command of the angel that came to me, I was not to know Mary until after the birth, and I had never seen a woman completely.

Just as my body urged me to dart out of the stable, she grabbed my forearm and squeezed with such force and wanting that I couldn't leave her side. The experience of the miracle of birth changed me. Such pain, suffering, and joy surrounded and filled my being.

As I held the perfectly formed, wet, and shiny little one in my calloused hands, I quickly reached for the cloth in our bundle and wiped Him clean. As He cried out at the night air, I held Him close to my breast while I covered Mary to keep her warm. Mary stared into my eyes and said, " I love you," without a word spoken. I returned the glance and looked down at the newborn.

He had settled down and looked up at me. I felt His warmth and worried that my work worn hands would offend His tender skin . . . until His tiny fingers wrapped around the edge of my hand and He fell asleep. I handed Him to Mary and she held Him close to her breast.

I was His father and He would be my boy! My joy was extreme. Jesus had come into my life like He would come into no others.

As we sat and enjoyed the smell of fresh hay, the clanking of the first Christmas bells hanging from our roommates the cattle, and as the light of stars and the moon filtered in, we felt peace.

Later that sleepless night shepherds came telling us that angels had sent them to see the Child of which the prophets had foretold.

We had laid Jesus in a manger, and as they peered in to see Him, they left raising their hands and praising God for the miracle.

After a time, we heard more Christmas bells. The bells of camels announced men of a royal caste, kings of eastern lands, bringing Jesus regal gifts of frankincense, myrrh, and gold. They were gracious and very impressed with the feeling of awe the Child emulated. We marveled after their visit.

That night an angel came to me in a dream and demanded we leave for Egypt immediately. I woke Mary and Jesus and we left before sunrise.

Why Egypt? Because that heathen Edomite, Herod, commanded that all male children in Israel, 2 years and younger, be slaughtered for fear that his high and mighty position of King was threatened. Herod died shortly thereafter and although Rachel still weeps for her children, no one wept for the tyrant Herod.

We then returned to Nazareth to raise Jesus and have a family.

My boy, Jesus, was the one to watch. His deep piercing blue eyes would soak up everything around Him. He wanted to know how everything worked. He loved to work with wood. I watched as He felt the wood, following the grain, using the tools to create, and how He inspected his finished product.

His first table was a catastrophe! As he looked over His design, one leg was shorter than the others and the top was far from smooth, He grimaced and looked at me and we shared a smile. He spent the rest of the day and into the night working to perfect His table.

Oh, there were the slivers!

One time, with tears streaming down His cheeks, He came to me and said, "Father, I need your help to get this sliver out to stop the pain." I obliged and after a hug and a kiss on the forehead He was back at the stool and working once again.

We laughed, learned, cried, and talked together.

As time went on, Jesus grew into a young man any father would be proud of. Oh, and He knew his scriptures . . . better than I did!

The time came to travel to the temple where Jesus would have an opportunity to ask questions to the teachers and rabbis of the temple. He was giddy as we traveled and high as a bird in the sky as we arrived and made arrangements. His eyes were eager to take in every sight, sound, and word.

As Mary and I watched Him ask His questions, I overheard the old ones against the back wall mutter, "Is this the carpenter's son? He is wise in his questioning and answers better than the rabbis."

My heart swelled with pride and I wanted to yell out, "That's my boy, Jesus!"

As we left, both Mary and I thought what an incredible experience it was to see our son in the temple asking questions and feeding on the word of God. Jesus had become a mensch . . . a person, a real person.

Terror filled Mary's voice as she ran up to me when we were almost back to Nazareth.

Mary exclaimed, "He's not with us!"

"What!"

We frantically searched every group and decided to head back to the temple. After a three day's journey and lots of sick feelings, we found Him in the temple with the same teachers and rabbis. But as we entered the room where he was, he didn't look up, He just continued to talk with the teachers.

He wasn't asking them, they were asking Him, and he was giving magnificent glorified answers.

We waited until they were done conversing and then approached Him. "Son, we were worried sick! How could you have done this to us?"

He turned to his mother and declared, "How is it that ye sought me? Wist ye not that I must be about my Father's business?"

It hit me like a spear through my heart. Most people of your day refer to me as His stepfather. I was His father until that declaration.

Oh, I loved him no less. We still embraced and talked, laughed, and cried together. But all the events of his birth, and the prophecies of the Messiah shot into my heart and it stopped for a moment. He is the Chosen One, the Holy One of Israel.

As I looked at Him, I could see his mother's softness. There was nothing of me in His features, but as I saw the light in His eyes, I knew in whose image His countenance was, and I loved Him for it. I could say no more. I pulled Him close and held Him tight. His warmth filled my soul and I knew He was right.

As I passed from this earthly existence to the next, I called each of my children to my side, youngest to eldest, and blessed them and gave them words of love and advice. As Jesus entered the room, He sat on the edge of my bed. His eyes were burning with glory and love as He looked at me.

"Father . . . ," He said, "I love you. You have given me so much! May my Father give you rest where you are going."

He held me in His arms as I passed to the other side. He wept as He kissed my cheek and said, "farewell, father."

As Jesus wrapped His fingers around my hand I was barely able to finish the words, "Till we meet again, my boy, . . . Jesus."

I watched from on high when He started his ministry . . . as He taught, healed, loved, and saved.

But the hardest time for me was when we all knew the time of His extreme suffering was at hand. There was to be an angel stand by His side in the Garden of Gethsemane. There was much discussion as to who should have the honor and privilege. I privately went to the Father and begged that I be the one to stand by this One whom I loved as my own.

The piercing, yet understanding, reply from the Father cut through my soul. "No! You love Him so much, you would intervene. He must do this on his own."

The Father and I went to the furthermost corner of eternity and yet His cries of agony and suffering still filled our ears. We held each other and wept together.

When He had finished His work, He approached His Father and they embraced. I heard the words, "My Beloved Son."

Warmth filled the heavens.

I thought He wouldn't notice me in the crowd. He walked towards me, His eyes filled with tears as His gaze met mine. He embraced me. He had big stout arms and He had grown tall and strong. His warmth filled my soul and I knew that it was right.

All is well.

So when Christmas comes, just know that the true sounds are the clanking bells of cattle, the still night breeze, and the bleating of sheep in the distance.

The true smells of Christmas are fresh hay, the charcoal smell of a small oil lamp, and of animals.

The true sights of Christmas are the lights of the sky and the light emanating from the eyes of a newborn.

Do you want to feel Christmas? Rub the cheek of a baby and let him hold your finger in his hand.

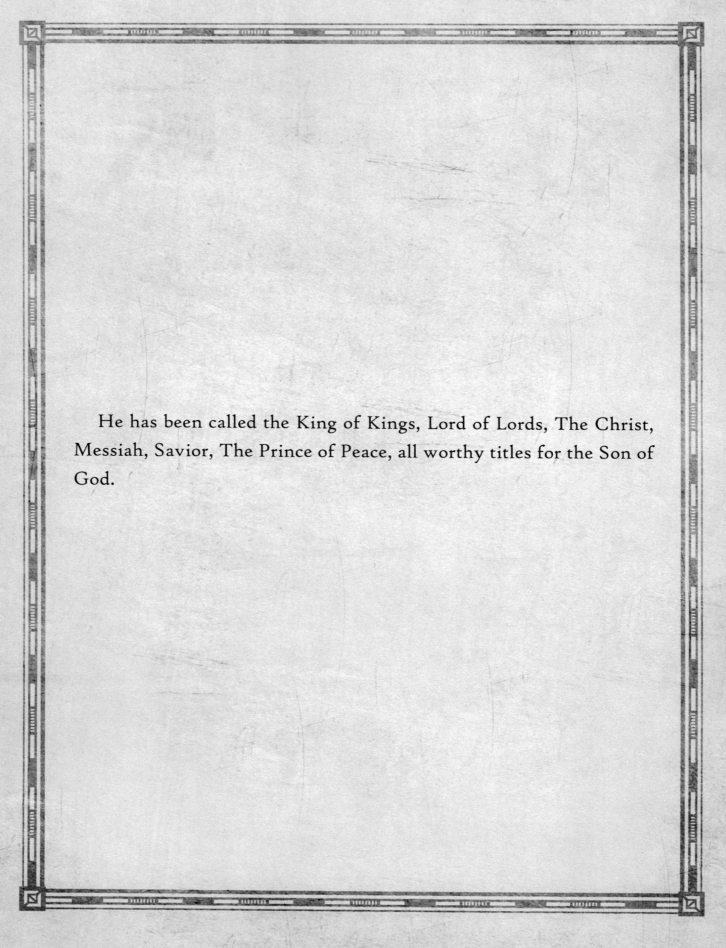

He has been called the King of Kings, Lord of Lords, The Christ, Messiah, Savior, The Prince of Peace, all worthy titles for the Son of God.

I call Him . . .

my Boy, Jesus.

Who knows what really goes on in my mind? I love to tell stories and I am always looking for opportunities to tell new ones. I have many original stories, but My Boy Jesus is the first of my stories that I have actually written down.

My wife Meg and I have been married for over 28 years and have not had television in our home. This has given us incredible opportunities to expand our storytelling and artistic talents. Evenings can be quite exciting in the Erekson home! We have established our family business, The Nutmeg Company (I am the nut and she is the Meg), to operate our artistic abilities.

Meg spent many months getting the right expressions, composition, and feeling into the drawings in this book. She is an art teacher extraordinaire and is a creator that includes emotion in all her art.

Before I wrote and performed My Boy Jesus, I have always thought and pondered about Joseph the stepfather of Jesus. I really wondered what it was like for Joseph, a dedicated Jewish man, to know that Mary's son was indeed the Son of God. I think Joseph must have had a great and tender love for Mary to be there helping with the birth of Jesus in such humble circumstances.

If anyone is interested in hiring Ted to come and tell this story, or any of his other stories you can contact him at nutmegco@gmail.com.